This journal belongs to

Introduction

Welcome to Unlocking Greatness Daily Gratitude Journal! This journal is especially made for your everyday planning and journaling.

Each day, a space is provided for you to write an affirmation. Sticking to your affirmation throughout the day will help you gain a more positive look in the things you do everyday.

A prompt section is also for you to write up about a particular prompt put each day. These prompts repeat throughout the journal in a cycle which will help you trace progress in the way you have your thoughts written down.

A Gratitude List is also on each day so you can write the things you are thankful for each day, giving you a positive vibe as the day goes along.

Finally, a section to write your plans and to-dos for the day is also in each daily page to let you be reminded of your daily priorities.

So, turn up this page and start your daily journey in writing. Have fun!

Date
____

S   M   T   W   T   F   S
◯   ◯   ◯   ◯   ◯   ◯   ◯

👀 Today's Affirmation

🖋 Today's Prompt

Today I am excited about...

____

____

____

____

____

____

____

____

♥ My Gratitude List

1 ___________________________

2 ___________________________

3 ___________________________

🔖 Notes | Plans | To-Do

Date
____

S   M   T   W   T   F   S
○   ○   ○   ○   ○   ○   ○

👓 Today's Affirmation

🖋 Today's Prompt

Today I am thankful...

____

____

____

____

____

____

____

____

♥ My Gratitude List

1 _______________________

2 _______________________

3 _______________________

🔖 Notes | Plans | To-Do

Date

S M T W T F S
○ ○ ○ ○ ○ ○ ○

👓 Today's Affirmation

🖊 Today's Prompt

Today, I'm growing through...

____
____
____
____
____
____
____
____

♥ My Gratitude List

1 _______________________

2 _______________________

3 _______________________

🔖 Notes | Plans | To-Do

Date
____

S   M   T   W   T   F   S
○   ○   ○   ○   ○   ○   ○

Today's Affirmation

Today's Prompt

Today, I overcame...

____

____

____

____

____

____

____

____

My Gratitude List

1 _______________________________

2 _______________________________

3 _______________________________

Notes | Plans | To-Do

Date

S M T W T F S
○ ○ ○ ○ ○ ○ ○

Today's Affirmation

Today's Prompt

Today, I learned that...

____
____
____
____
____
____
____
____

♥ My Gratitude List

1 ___________________________

2 ___________________________

3 ___________________________

Notes | Plans | To-Do

Date
____

S   M   T   W   T   F   S
○   ○   ○   ○   ○   ○   ○

👀 Today's Affirmation

✍ Today's Prompt

Today, I'm ecstatic about...

____

____

____

____

____

____

____

____

♥ My Gratitude List

🔖 Notes | Plans | To-Do

1
____

2
____

3
____

Date
____

S   M   T   W   T   F   S

○   ○   ○   ○   ○   ○   ○

👁 Today's Affirmation

✍ Today's Prompt

Today I am working on...

____

____

____

____

____

____

____

____

♥ My Gratitude List

🔖 Notes | Plans | To-Do

1
____

2
____

3
____

Date
____

S   M   T   W   T   F   S
○   ○   ○   ○   ○   ○   ○

💬 Today's Affirmation

🖋 Today's Prompt

Today I am excited about...

____
____
____
____
____
____
____
____

♥ My Gratitude List

🔖 Notes | Plans | To-Do

1 _______________________________________

2 _______________________________________

3 _______________________________________

Date

S   M   T   W   T   F   S
○   ○   ○   ○   ○   ○   ○

Today's Affirmation

Today's Prompt

Today I am thankful...

____
____
____
____
____
____
____
____

♥ My Gratitude List

1 _______________________________

2 _______________________________

3 _______________________________

🔖 Notes | Plans | To-Do

Date
____

S   M   T   W   T   F   S
○   ○   ○   ○   ○   ○   ○

👀 Today's Affirmation

🖊 Today's Prompt

Today, I'm growing through...

____
____
____
____
____
____
____
____

♥ My Gratitude List

🔖 Notes | Plans | To-Do

1 _______________________________

2 _______________________________

3 _______________________________

Date
____

S   M   T   W   T   F   S
O   O   O   O   O   O   O

👀 Today's Affirmation

🖋 Today's Prompt

Today, I overcame...

____

____

____

____

____

____

____

____

♥ My Gratitude List

🔖 Notes | Plans | To-Do

1 ______________________

2 ______________________

3 ______________________

Date

S   M   T   W   T   F   S

○   ○   ○   ○   ○   ○   ○

🗣 Today's Affirmation

🖋 Today's Prompt

Today, I learned that...

♥ My Gratitude List

1

2

3

🔖 Notes | Plans | To-Do

Date
____

S   M   T   W   T   F   S
○   ○   ○   ○   ○   ○   ○

👀 Today's Affirmation

✍ Today's Prompt

Today, I'm ecstatic about...

____
____
____
____
____
____
____
____
____

♥ My Gratitude List

🔖 Notes | Plans | To-Do

1 _______________________________

2 _______________________________

3 _______________________________

Date
____

S   M   T   W   T   F   S
○   ○   ○   ○   ○   ○   ○

👐 Today's Affirmation

🖊 Today's Prompt

Today I am working on...

____

____

____

____

____

____

____

____

❤ My Gratitude List

1
____

2
____

3
____

🔖 Notes | Plans | To-Do

Date

S   M   T   W   T   F   S
○   ○   ○   ○   ○   ○   ○

👓 Today's Affirmation

🖊 Today's Prompt

Today I am excited about...

____

____

____

____

____

____

____

____

♥ My Gratitude List

1 _______________________________

2 _______________________________

3 _______________________________

🔖 Notes | Plans | To-Do

Date
____

S   M   T   W   T   F   S
O   O   O   O   O   O   O

Today's Affirmation

Today's Prompt

Today I am thankful...

____

____

____

____

____

____

____

____

♥ My Gratitude List

🔖 Notes | Plans | To-Do

1
____

2
____

3
____

Date
____

S   M   T   W   T   F   S
○   ○   ○   ○   ○   ○   ○

Today's Affirmation

Today's Prompt

Today, I'm growing through...

____

____

____

____

____

____

____

____

♥ My Gratitude List

🔖 Notes | Plans | To-Do

1 _______________________

2 _______________________

3 _______________________

Date
____

S   M   T   W   T   F   S
○   ○   ○   ○   ○   ○   ○

👁 Today's Affirmation

✍ Today's Prompt

Today, I overcame...

____
____
____
____
____
____
____
____

♥ My Gratitude List

1
____

2
____

3
____

🔖 Notes | Plans | To-Do

Date
____

S   M   T   W   T   F   S
○   ○   ○   ○   ○   ○   ○

👓 Today's Affirmation

✒ Today's Prompt

Today, I learned that...

____

____

____

____

____

____

____

____

♥ My Gratitude List

1 _______________________

2 _______________________

3 _______________________

🔖 Notes | Plans | To-Do

Date
____

S M T W T F S
◯ ◯ ◯ ◯ ◯ ◯ ◯

👓 Today's Affirmation

✎ Today's Prompt

Today, I'm ecstatic about...

____
____
____
____
____
____
____
____

♥ My Gratitude List

1 _______________________

2 _______________________

3 _______________________

🔖 Notes | Plans | To-Do

Date
____

S   M   T   W   T   F   S
○   ○   ○   ○   ○   ○   ○

Today's Affirmation

Today's Prompt

Today I am working on...

____
____
____
____
____
____
____
____

♥ My Gratitude List

1 ______________________________

2 ______________________________

3 ______________________________

⚑ Notes | Plans | To-Do

Date
____

S   M   T   W   T   F   S
◯   ◯   ◯   ◯   ◯   ◯   ◯

💬 Today's Affirmation

✒ Today's Prompt

Today I am excited about...

____

____

____

____

____

____

____

____

🖤 My Gratitude List

🔖 Notes | Plans | To-Do

1
____

2
____

3
____

Date
____

S   M   T   W   T   F   S
○   ○   ○   ○   ○   ○   ○

👀 Today's Affirmation

🖋 Today's Prompt

Today I am thankful...

____
____
____
____
____
____
____
____

♥ My Gratitude List

1 _________________________________

2 _________________________________

3 _________________________________

🔖 Notes | Plans | To-Do

Date
____

S   M   T   W   T   F   S
○   ○   ○   ○   ○   ○   ○

👓 Today's Affirmation

🖋 Today's Prompt

Today, I'm growing through...

____
____
____
____
____
____
____
____

❤ My Gratitude List

1
____

2
____

3
____

🔖 Notes | Plans | To-Do

Date

S   M   T   W   T   F   S
〇 〇 〇 〇 〇 〇 〇

👓 Today's Affirmation

🖋 Today's Prompt

Today, I overcame...

____

____

____

____

____

____

____

____

♥ My Gratitude List

1 _______________________________

2 _______________________________

3 _______________________________

🔖 Notes | Plans | To-Do

Date
____

| S | M | T | W | T | F | S |
| ○ | ○ | ○ | ○ | ○ | ○ | ○ |

👀 Today's Affirmation

🖋 Today's Prompt

Today, I learned that...

____
____
____
____
____
____
____
____

♥ My Gratitude List

🔖 Notes | Plans | To-Do

1 _______________________

2 _______________________

3 _______________________

Date
____

S   M   T   W   T   F   S
◯   ◯   ◯   ◯   ◯   ◯   ◯

Today's Affirmation

Today's Prompt

Today, I'm ecstatic about...

____
____
____
____
____
____
____
____

♥ My Gratitude List

1 _______________________

2 _______________________

3 _______________________

🔖 Notes | Plans | To-Do

Date
____

S   M   T   W   T   F   S
◯ ◯ ◯ ◯ ◯ ◯ ◯

👀 Today's Affirmation

🖊 Today's Prompt

Today I am working on...

____

____

____

____

____

____

____

____

🖤 My Gratitude List

🔖 Notes | Plans | To-Do

1
____

2
____

3
____

Date
____

S   M   T   W   T   F   S
○   ○   ○   ○   ○   ○   ○

∞ Today's Affirmation

✒ Today's Prompt

Today I am excited about...

____

____

____

____

____

____

____

____

♥ My Gratitude List

🔖 Notes | Plans | To-Do

1 _______________________

2 _______________________

3 _______________________

Date
____

S   M   T   W   T   F   S
◯   ◯   ◯   ◯   ◯   ◯   ◯

👓 Today's Affirmation

🖋 Today's Prompt

Today I am thankful...

____
____
____
____
____
____
____
____

♥ My Gratitude List

1 _______________________________

2 _______________________________

3 _______________________________

🔖 Notes | Plans | To-Do

Date

S   M   T   W   T   F   S
○   ○   ○   ○   ○   ○   ○

👓 Today's Affirmation

🖋 Today's Prompt

Today, I'm growing through...

____
____
____
____
____
____
____
____
____

♥ My Gratitude List

1 _______________________________

2 _______________________________

3 _______________________________

🔖 Notes | Plans | To-Do

Date
____

S   M   T   W   T   F   S
◯   ◯   ◯   ◯   ◯   ◯   ◯

👓 Today's Affirmation

🖋 Today's Prompt

Today, I overcame...

____
____
____
____
____
____
____
____

♥ My Gratitude List

🔖 Notes | Plans | To-Do

1
____

2
____

3
____

Date _______________

S   M   T   W   T   F   S
○   ○   ○   ○   ○   ○   ○

👀 Today's Affirmation

🖊 Today's Prompt

Today, I learned that...

____

____

____

____

____

____

____

____

____

♥ My Gratitude List

🔖 Notes | Plans | To-Do

1 _______________________________

2 _______________________________

3 _______________________________

Date
____
S   M   T   W   T   F   S
◯   ◯   ◯   ◯   ◯   ◯   ◯

🙾 Today's Affirmation

🖋 Today's Prompt

Today, I'm ecstatic about...

____
____
____
____
____
____
____
____

♥ My Gratitude List

🔖 Notes | Plans | To-Do

1
____

2
____

3
____

Date
____

S   M   T   W   T   F   S
◯ ◯ ◯ ◯ ◯ ◯ ◯

👁 Today's Affirmation

✍ Today's Prompt

Today I am working on...

____

____

____

____

____

____

____

____

♥ My Gratitude List

1 ______________________________

2 ______________________________

3 ______________________________

🔖 Notes | Plans | To-Do

Date
____

S   M   T   W   T   F   S
◯   ◯   ◯   ◯   ◯   ◯   ◯

Today's Affirmation

Today's Prompt

Today I am excited about...

____
____
____
____
____
____
____
____

♥ My Gratitude List

Notes | Plans | To-Do

1
____

2
____

3
____

Date

S   M   T   W   T   F   S
〇 〇 〇 〇 〇 〇 〇

◕ Today's Affirmation

✍ Today's Prompt

Today I am thankful...

____

____

____

____

____

____

____

____

♥ My Gratitude List

▐ Notes | Plans | To-Do

1 _______________________________

2 _______________________________

3 _______________________________

Date
____

S   M   T   W   T   F   S
○   ○   ○   ○   ○   ○   ○

👓 Today's Affirmation

🖋 Today's Prompt

Today, I'm growing through...

____
____
____
____
____
____
____
____

♥ My Gratitude List

1 _____________________________

2 _____________________________

3 _____________________________

🔖 Notes | Plans | To-Do

Date

S M T W T F S
○ ○ ○ ○ ○ ○ ○

👓 Today's Affirmation

🖋 Today's Prompt

Today, I overcame...

____

____

____

____

____

____

____

____

♥ My Gratitude List

🔖 Notes | Plans | To-Do

1
____

2
____

3
____

Date
____

S   M   T   W   T   F   S

◯ ◯ ◯ ◯ ◯ ◯ ◯

👓 Today's Affirmation

🖊 Today's Prompt

Today, I learned that...

____

____

____

____

____

____

____

____

♥ My Gratitude List

🔖 Notes | Plans | To-Do

1 ______________________________

2 ______________________________

3 ______________________________

Date
____

S   M   T   W   T   F   S
○   ○   ○   ○   ○   ○   ○

👁 Today's Affirmation

✒ Today's Prompt

Today, I'm ecstatic about...

____
____
____
____
____
____
____
____
____

♥ My Gratitude List

1 _______________________________

2 _______________________________

3 _______________________________

🔖 Notes | Plans | To-Do

Date

S M T W T F S
○ ○ ○ ○ ○ ○ ○

👁 Today's Affirmation

✒ Today's Prompt

Today I am working on...

____

____

____

____

____

____

____

____

♥ My Gratitude List

1
____

2
____

3
____

🔖 Notes | Plans | To-Do

Date
____

S   M   T   W   T   F   S
○   ○   ○   ○   ○   ○   ○

👓 Today's Affirmation

🏃 Today's Prompt

Today I am excited about...

____
____
____
____
____
____
____
____
____

♥ My Gratitude List

🔖 Notes | Plans | To-Do

1
____

2
____

3
____

Date
____

S   M   T   W   T   F   S
O   O   O   O   O   O   O

💬 Today's Affirmation

🖊 Today's Prompt

Today I am thankful...

____
____
____
____
____
____
____
____

♥ My Gratitude List

1
____

2
____

3
____

🔖 Notes | Plans | To-Do

Date
____

S   M   T   W   T   F   S
○   ○   ○   ○   ○   ○   ○

👀 Today's Affirmation

✍ Today's Prompt

Today, I'm growing through...

____
____
____
____
____
____
____
____
____

♥ My Gratitude List

1
____

2
____

3
____

🔖 Notes | Plans | To-Do

Date
____

S　M　T　W　T　F　S
○　○　○　○　○　○　○

💬 Today's Affirmation

✒ Today's Prompt

Today, I overcame...

____
____
____
____
____
____
____
____

♥ My Gratitude List

1
____

2
____

3
____

🔖 Notes | Plans | To-Do

Date

S   M   T   W   T   F   S
○   ○   ○   ○   ○   ○   ○

👓 Today's Affirmation

🖊 Today's Prompt

Today, I learned that...

____

____

____

____

____

____

____

____

♥ My Gratitude List

1 _______________________________

2 _______________________________

3 _______________________________

🔖 Notes | Plans | To-Do

Date
____

S   M   T   W   T   F   S
O   O   O   O   O   O   O

⬤ Today's Affirmation

🖊 Today's Prompt

Today, I'm ecstatic about...

____

____

____

____

____

____

____

____

♥ My Gratitude List

1 _______________________

2 _______________________

3 _______________________

🔖 Notes | Plans | To-Do

Date
____

S   M   T   W   T   F   S
○   ○   ○   ○   ○   ○   ○

👀 Today's Affirmation

🖋 Today's Prompt

Today I am working on...

____

____

____

____

____

____

____

____

♥ My Gratitude List

🔖 Notes | Plans | To-Do

1 _______________________

2 _______________________

3 _______________________

Date
____

S   M   T   W   T   F   S
○   ○   ○   ○   ○   ○   ○

🗣 Today's Affirmation

✏ Today's Prompt

Today I am excited about...

____
____
____
____
____
____
____
____

♥ My Gratitude List

🔖 Notes | Plans | To-Do

1 _______________________________

2 _______________________________

3 _______________________________

Date

S   M   T   W   T   F   S
○ ○ ○ ○ ○ ○ ○

∞ Today's Affirmation

✒ Today's Prompt

Today I am thankful...

____

____

____

____

____

____

____

____

♥ My Gratitude List

1 ______________________________

2 ______________________________

3 ______________________________

🔖 Notes | Plans | To-Do

Date
____

S   M   T   W   T   F   S
O   O   O   O   O   O   O

💬 Today's Affirmation

✒ Today's Prompt

Today, I'm growing through...

____

____

____

____

____

____

____

____

♥ My Gratitude List

1 _______________________________

2 _______________________________

3 _______________________________

🔖 Notes | Plans | To-Do

Date
____

S M T W T F S
○ ○ ○ ○ ○ ○ ○

🗨 Today's Affirmation

✍ Today's Prompt

Today, I overcame...

____

____

____

____

____

____

____

____

♥ My Gratitude List

🔖 Notes | Plans | To-Do

1
____

2
____

3
____

Date
____

S   M   T   W   T   F   S
O   O   O   O   O   O   O

👓 Today's Affirmation

🖋 Today's Prompt

Today, I learned that...

____
____
____
____
____
____
____
____

♥ My Gratitude List

1 _____________________________

2 _____________________________

3 _____________________________

🔖 Notes | Plans | To-Do

Date
____

S   M   T   W   T   F   S
○   ○   ○   ○   ○   ○   ○

Today's Affirmation

Today's Prompt

Today, I'm ecstatic about...

____
____
____
____
____
____
____
____

♥ My Gratitude List

1 ____________________

2 ____________________

3 ____________________

▐ Notes | Plans | To-Do

Date
____

S   M   T   W   T   F   S
◯ ◯ ◯ ◯ ◯ ◯ ◯

Today's Affirmation

Today's Prompt

Today I am working on...

____

____

____

____

____

____

____

____

♥ My Gratitude List

1 _______________________

2 _______________________

3 _______________________

▐ Notes | Plans | To-Do

Date

S   M   T   W   T   F   S
◯   ◯   ◯   ◯   ◯   ◯   ◯

👀 Today's Affirmation

🖋 Today's Prompt

Today I am excited about...

____
____
____
____
____
____
____
____
____

🖤 My Gratitude List

1 _______________________________

2 _______________________________

3 _______________________________

🔖 Notes | Plans | To-Do

Date

S   M   T   W   T   F   S
O   O   O   O   O   O   O

Today's Affirmation

Today's Prompt

Today I am thankful...

____

____

____

____

____

____

____

____

♥ My Gratitude List

1 _____________________________

2 _____________________________

3 _____________________________

Notes | Plans | To-Do

Date
____

S   M   T   W   T   F   S
◯   ◯   ◯   ◯   ◯   ◯   ◯

∞ Today's Affirmation

🖋 Today's Prompt

Today, I'm growing through...

____

____

____

____

____

____

____

____

♥ My Gratitude List

1 _______________________________

2 _______________________________

3 _______________________________

🔖 Notes | Plans | To-Do

Date

S M T W T F S
○ ○ ○ ○ ○ ○ ○

💬 Today's Affirmation

🖋 Today's Prompt

Today, I overcame...

____

____

____

____

____

____

____

____

♥ My Gratitude List

1 ____________________________

2 ____________________________

3 ____________________________

🔖 Notes | Plans | To-Do

Date
____

S   M   T   W   T   F   S
○   ○   ○   ○   ○   ○   ○

👀 Today's Affirmation

🖊 Today's Prompt

Today, I learned that...

____
____
____
____
____
____
____
____
____

♥ My Gratitude List

1 _______________________

2 _______________________

3 _______________________

🔖 Notes | Plans | To-Do

Date
____

S   M   T   W   T   F   S
○   ○   ○   ○   ○   ○   ○

👓 Today's Affirmation

🖋 Today's Prompt

Today, I'm ecstatic about...

____
____
____
____
____
____
____
____
____

♥ My Gratitude List

1 ___________________________

2 ___________________________

3 ___________________________

🔖 Notes | Plans | To-Do

Date
____

S   M   T   W   T   F   S
◯   ◯   ◯   ◯   ◯   ◯   ◯

⚭ Today's Affirmation

✒ Today's Prompt

Today I am working on...

____
____
____
____
____
____
____
____

♥ My Gratitude List

1 ____________________________

2 ____________________________

3 ____________________________

🔖 Notes | Plans | To-Do

Date
____

S   M   T   W   T   F   S
○   ○   ○   ○   ○   ○   ○

👀 Today's Affirmation

✒ Today's Prompt

Today I am excited about...

____
____
____
____
____
____
____
____

♥ My Gratitude List

1 _______________________________

2 _______________________________

3 _______________________________

🔖 Notes | Plans | To-Do

Date __________________

S   M   T   W   T   F   S
○   ○   ○   ○   ○   ○   ○

Today's Affirmation

Today's Prompt

Today I am thankful...

____

____

____

____

____

____

____

____

♥ My Gratitude List

▉ Notes | Plans | To-Do

1 __________________________

2 __________________________

3 __________________________

Date
____

S   M   T   W   T   F   S
○   ○   ○   ○   ○   ○   ○

🗩 Today's Affirmation

🖋 Today's Prompt

Today, I'm growing through...

____
____
____
____
____
____
____
____

♥ My Gratitude List

1 _____________________________

2 _____________________________

3 _____________________________

🔖 Notes | Plans | To-Do

Date

S   M   T   W   T   F   S
O   O   O   O   O   O   O

😇 Today's Affirmation

🖊 Today's Prompt

Today, I overcame...

____

____

____

____

____

____

____

____

♥ My Gratitude List

1 _______________________________

2 _______________________________

3 _______________________________

🔖 Notes | Plans | To-Do

Date
____

| S | M | T | W | T | F | S |
| ○ | ○ | ○ | ○ | ○ | ○ | ○ |

👓 Today's Affirmation

🖋 Today's Prompt

Today, I learned that...

____
____
____
____
____
____
____
____

♥ My Gratitude List

1 _______________________________

2 _______________________________

3 _______________________________

🔖 Notes | Plans | To-Do

Date
____

S   M   T   W   T   F   S
O   O   O   O   O   O   O

👀 Today's Affirmation

🖊 Today's Prompt

Today, I'm ecstatic about...

____
____
____
____
____
____
____
____

♥ My Gratitude List

1 ____________________________

2 ____________________________

3 ____________________________

🔖 Notes | Plans | To-Do

Date
____

S   M   T   W   T   F   S
◯   ◯   ◯   ◯   ◯   ◯   ◯

👓 Today's Affirmation

🖋 Today's Prompt

Today I am working on...

____

____

____

____

____

____

____

____

♥ My Gratitude List

1 _____________________________

2 _____________________________

3 _____________________________

🔖 Notes | Plans | To-Do

Date

S   M   T   W   T   F   S
O   O   O   O   O   O   O

👀 Today's Affirmation

🖋 Today's Prompt

Today I am excited about...

____

____

____

____

____

____

____

♥ My Gratitude List

1 ______________________________

2 ______________________________

3 ______________________________

🔖 Notes | Plans | To-Do

Date
____

S   M   T   W   T   F   S
O   O   O   O   O   O   O

💬 Today's Affirmation

✒ Today's Prompt

Today I am thankful...

____
____
____
____
____
____
____
____

♥ My Gratitude List

1 _______________________________

2 _______________________________

3 _______________________________

🔖 Notes | Plans | To-Do

Date
____

S   M   T   W   T   F   S
◯   ◯   ◯   ◯   ◯   ◯   ◯

👓 Today's Affirmation

🖋 Today's Prompt

Today, I'm growing through...

____
____
____
____
____
____
____
____

♥ My Gratitude List

🔖 Notes | Plans | To-Do

1
____

2
____

3
____

Date
____

S   M   T   W   T   F   S
◯   ◯   ◯   ◯   ◯   ◯   ◯

👀 Today's Affirmation

✍ Today's Prompt

Today, I overcame...

____
____
____
____
____
____
____
____

♥ My Gratitude List

1 _____________________________

2 _____________________________

3 _____________________________

🔖 Notes | Plans | To-Do

Date
____

S   M   T   W   T   F   S
○   ○   ○   ○   ○   ○   ○

👀 Today's Affirmation

🖋 Today's Prompt

Today, I learned that...

____
____
____
____
____
____
____
____

♥ My Gratitude List

🔖 Notes | Plans | To-Do

1 _____________________________

2 _____________________________

3 _____________________________

Date
____

S M T W T F S
○ ○ ○ ○ ○ ○ ○

👀 Today's Affirmation

🖊 Today's Prompt

Today, I'm ecstatic about...

____
____
____
____
____
____
____
____

♥ My Gratitude List

🔖 Notes | Plans | To-Do

1 _______________________

2 _______________________

3 _______________________

Date
____

S M T W T F S
○ ○ ○ ○ ○ ○ ○

👀 Today's Affirmation

🖊 Today's Prompt

Today I am working on...

____

____

____

____

____

____

____

____

♥ My Gratitude List

1
____

2
____

3
____

🔖 Notes | Plans | To-Do

Date
____

S   M   T   W   T   F   S
O   O   O   O   O   O   O

👀 Today's Affirmation

✒ Today's Prompt

Today I am excited about...

____
____
____
____
____
____
____
____

♥ My Gratitude List

🔖 Notes | Plans | To-Do

1
____

2
____

3
____

Date

S　M　T　W　T　F　S
○　○　○　○　○　○　○

👁 Today's Affirmation

🖋 Today's Prompt

Today I am thankful...

____

____

____

____

____

____

____

____

♥ My Gratitude List

1 _______________________________

2 _______________________________

3 _______________________________

🔖 Notes | Plans | To-Do

Date
____

S   M   T   W   T   F   S
○   ○   ○   ○   ○   ○   ○

🧿 **Today's Affirmation**

🖋 **Today's Prompt**

Today, I'm growing through…

____
____
____
____
____
____
____
____

♥ **My Gratitude List**

🔖 **Notes | Plans | To-Do**

1 _______________________________

2 _______________________________

3 _______________________________

Date
____

S   M   T   W   T   F   S
○   ○   ○   ○   ○   ○   ○

👀 Today's Affirmation

✍ Today's Prompt

Today, I overcame...

____
____
____
____
____
____
____
____

♥ My Gratitude List

1
____

2
____

3
____

🔖 Notes | Plans | To-Do

Date

S M T W T F S
○ ○ ○ ○ ○ ○ ○

👀 Today's Affirmation

🖋 Today's Prompt

Today, I learned that...

____
____
____
____
____
____
____
____

♥ My Gratitude List

1 _______________________________

2 _______________________________

3 _______________________________

🔖 Notes | Plans | To-Do

Date
____

S   M   T   W   T   F   S
◯   ◯   ◯   ◯   ◯   ◯   ◯

👀 Today's Affirmation

🖊 Today's Prompt

Today, I'm ecstatic about...

____
____
____
____
____
____
____
____

♥ My Gratitude List

1
____

2
____

3
____

🔖 Notes | Plans | To-Do

Date
____

S   M   T   W   T   F   S
○   ○   ○   ○   ○   ○   ○

Today's Affirmation

Today's Prompt

Today I am working on...

____
____
____
____
____
____
____
____

♥ My Gratitude List

▥ Notes | Plans | To-Do

1
____

2
____

3
____

Date
____

S   M   T   W   T   F   S
◯   ◯   ◯   ◯   ◯   ◯   ◯

👓 Today's Affirmation

🖋 Today's Prompt

Today I am excited about...

____

____

____

____

____

____

____

____

____

♥ My Gratitude List

1 _______________________

2 _______________________

3 _______________________

🔖 Notes | Plans | To-Do

Date
____

S   M   T   W   T   F   S
○   ○   ○   ○   ○   ○   ○

👀 Today's Affirmation

🖋 Today's Prompt

Today I am thankful...

____
____
____
____
____
____
____
____

♥ My Gratitude List

1
____

2
____

3
____

🔖 Notes | Plans | To-Do

Date ______________

S M T W T F S
◯ ◯ ◯ ◯ ◯ ◯ ◯

Today's Affirmation

Today's Prompt

Today, I'm growing through...

____
____
____
____
____
____
____
____
____

♥ My Gratitude List

1
____

2
____

3
____

🔖 Notes | Plans | To-Do

Date ___________

S M T W T F S
○ ○ ○ ○ ○ ○ ○

💬 Today's Affirmation

✍ Today's Prompt

Today, I overcame...

____
____
____
____
____
____
____
____

♥ My Gratitude List

1 _________________________________

2 _________________________________

3 _________________________________

🔖 Notes | Plans | To-Do

Date
____

S   M   T   W   T   F   S
○   ○   ○   ○   ○   ○   ○

👀 Today's Affirmation

🖋 Today's Prompt

Today, I learned that...

____
____
____
____
____
____
____
____

❤ My Gratitude List

🔖 Notes | Plans | To-Do

1
____

2
____

3
____

Date
____

S   M   T   W   T   F   S
○   ○   ○   ○   ○   ○   ○

👓 Today's Affirmation

✒ Today's Prompt

Today, I'm ecstatic about...

____

____

____

____

____

____

____

____

♥ My Gratitude List

🔖 Notes | Plans | To-Do

1
____

2
____

3
____

Date
____

S   M   T   W   T   F   S
○   ○   ○   ○   ○   ○   ○

◎ Today's Affirmation

🖋 Today's Prompt

Today I am working on...

____

____

____

____

____

____

____

____

♥ My Gratitude List

1
____

2
____

3
____

🔖 Notes | Plans | To-Do

Date

S   M   T   W   T   F   S
○   ○   ○   ○   ○   ○   ○

👁 Today's Affirmation

🖋 Today's Prompt

Today I am excited about...

____
____
____
____
____
____
____
____

♥ My Gratitude List

1 _______________________________

2 _______________________________

3 _______________________________

🔖 Notes | Plans | To-Do

Date
____

S   M   T   W   T   F   S
○   ○   ○   ○   ○   ○   ○

👓 Today's Affirmation

🖋 Today's Prompt

Today I am thankful...

____
____
____
____
____
____
____
____
____

♥ My Gratitude List

1 _______________________________

2 _______________________________

3 _______________________________

🔖 Notes | Plans | To-Do

Date
____

S   M   T   W   T   F   S
○   ○   ○   ○   ○   ○   ○

💬 Today's Affirmation

🖋 Today's Prompt

Today, I'm growing through...

____
____
____
____
____
____
____
____

🖤 My Gratitude List

🔖 Notes | Plans | To-Do

1
____

2
____

3
____

Date
____

S   M   T   W   T   F   S
O   O   O   O   O   O   O

👀 Today's Affirmation

🖊 Today's Prompt

Today, I overcame…

____
____
____
____
____
____
____
____

♥ My Gratitude List

🔖 Notes | Plans | To-Do

1
____

2
____

3
____

Date
____

S   M   T   W   T   F   S
O   O   O   O   O   O   O

💬 Today's Affirmation

✒ Today's Prompt

Today, I learned that...

____
____
____
____
____
____
____
____

♥ My Gratitude List

🔖 Notes | Plans | To-Do

1
____

2
____

3
____

Date

S   M   T   W   T   F   S
○   ○   ○   ○   ○   ○   ○

Today's Affirmation

Today's Prompt

Today, I'm ecstatic about...

____

____

____

____

____

____

____

____

♥ My Gratitude List

⚑ Notes | Plans | To-Do

1
____

2
____

3
____

Date
____

S   M   T   W   T   F   S
◯   ◯   ◯   ◯   ◯   ◯   ◯

👀 Today's Affirmation

✎ Today's Prompt

Today I am working on...

____
____
____
____
____
____
____
____

♥ My Gratitude List

1 _______________________________

2 _______________________________

3 _______________________________

🔖 Notes | Plans | To-Do

ABOUT THE
Author

LaDonna Marie is an International Multi -Award Winning Bestselling Author, Pastor, Speaker, Mother of Two and CEO of Nonprofit Planting Positive Seeds. Her purpose is to empower and encourage others in overcoming obstacles in life.
Her motto is to empower, encourage and motivate others to take action in their life and discover their champion inside. It's a part of her mission to reach individuals all over to the world and to assist them to LEAP into their greatness.

Pastor LaDonna's latest accomplishments in 2021 she was honored in the Top 20 National Authors of the Year by K.I.S.H Magazine, Honorable Ambassador for Planting Positive Seeds Nonprofit by Business Empowered Mississippi, Top Nonprofit in Mississippi by Mississippi Business Journal, Top 24 Trailblazers on the Move & Top Global Influencers in K.I.S.H. Magazine, . In 2021 she was the Speak up Radio Firebird Book Award Winner for Things I Wish I Knew and Honorable Mention for the New York Book Festival for The Journey/ The Path. In 2022 she was honored in the Top 15 Women Standing on God's Promise in Refuse to Lose Magazine.

For additional information visit Website www.ladonnamarie.org/shop and plantingpositiveseeds.com.

Books

BY THE AUTHOR

- Expressions of the Mind, Body and Soul
- Until Tomorrow Comes
- Lessons Shattered Pieces Being Restored
- Quiet Moments with God: 31 days of Life Lessons
- Eloquent Love Notes
- Lessons II Mirror Conversations
- Rebuilding Fragments Workbook
- Larry the Alligator: Makes Friends
- Quiet Moments with God: 21 Days of Positive Inspirations
- Maximizing Your Inner Strength Workbook
- Things I wish I Knew: Letters to My Little Sisters
- The Journey/ The Path : The Way I See It

All books can be purchased at www.ladonnamarie.org/shop